A SZÁMOK TÖRTÉNETE

THE NUMBER STORY

SMALL BOOK ONE

ENGLISH - HUNGARIAN

*Numbers Teach Children
Their Number Names*

written and illustrated by

MISS ANNA

Early Reader Edition of *The Number Story 1*
Bronze Medal Winner, 2016 Wishing Shelf Book Award

Library of Congress Control Number: 2018902040

Names: Miss Anna, author.
Title: Number story : numbers teach children their number names / Miss Anna.
Description: Portland, OR: Lumpy Publishing, 2018.
Identifiers: ISBN 978-1-945977-17-6 | LCCN 2018902040
Summary: The pictures and rhymes present stories which introduce numbers 0-10.
Subjects: LCSH Numeration—English--Hungarian--Pictorial works--Juvenile literature. | BISAC JUVENILE NONFICTION /
Languages: English--Hungarian
Classification: LCC QA141.3 .M57 2018 | DDC 513—dc23

Publisher: Lumpy Publishing
Website: www.missannabooks.com
Email: missanna@missannabooks.com

Paperback: ISBN 978-1-945977-17-6
Printed in the U.S.A.   1 3 5 7 9 10 8 6 4 2

Meg akarod tanulni a számok nevét?

It is very easy and a lot of fun!

Nagyon könnyű és nagyon szórakoztató!

Say-along our little jingle

Énekeld velünk piciny történetünk!

starting from Number One!

Kezdjük az egyes Számmal!

ONE looks like my one finger.

EGY

Egyenes, mint az ujjam.

1
ONE!
EGY!

2

TWO trails a tail.

KETTŐ

Egy farkinca követi.

A TAIL! EGY FARKINCA!

THREE   has bumps.

HÁROM

Olyan, mint egy domb.

Nézd a zöld dombokat!

4

FOUR carries a sail.

NÉGY

Ez egy vitorlás hajó.

A SAIL!
EGY VITORLA!

5

FIVE   is a racing track.

ÖT

Ez egy versenypálya.

VROOM
ZÜMMM!

SIX curves like a snail.

HAT

Hajlik, mint egy csiga.

A SNAIL!   EGY CSIGA!

7

SEVEN has a sharp angle.

HÉT

Ez egy fejsze.

BE CAREFUL! IT'S SHARP!
Légy óvatos! Éles!

8

EIGHT is rollercoaster rails.

NYOLC

Ez egy hullámvasút.

JUHÉÉ!
YIPPEE!

NINE   is a bubble on a stick.

KILENC

Ez egy buborék egy boton.

A BUBBLE! EGY BUBORÉK!

TEN   is an eye of a whale.

TÍZ

Ez egy bálna egyik szeme.

WINK!
KACSINT!
HELLO! HELLÓ!

And
És
0
ZERO   is an empty pail.
NULLA
Ez egy üres vödör.

IT'S
EMPTY!
ÜRES!

Thank you for playing with us today.

We had a lot of fun too!

Köszönjük, hogy velünk játszottál.

Mi is jót szórakoztunk!

We are your Number friends,
Zero to Ten,
Who will be here for you~

A barátaid vagyunk
Nullától Tízig.

Mindig veletek leszünk.

Bye-bye now!
See you again soon.

Szia!

Hamarosan újra találkozunk!

The Numbers are *SINGING* too!

To sing-a-long, look for Miss Anna Number Story
at your favorite music store like iTUNES.

MP3

Numbers 0-10
IDENTIFYING
& COUNTING

Numbers 11-20
& Ordinals
first, second, third…

Numbers 0-100
& Place Values
ones, tens, hundreds…

About Clocks
& Telling Time
hours, minutes, seconds

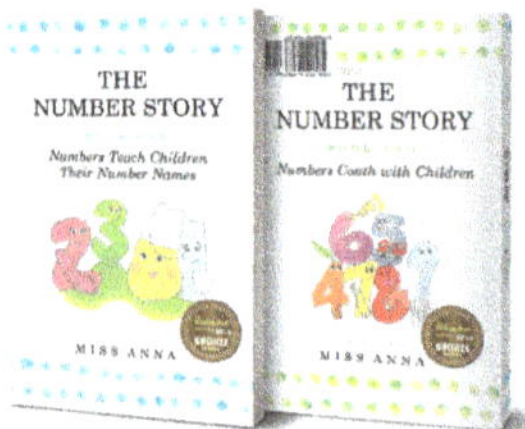

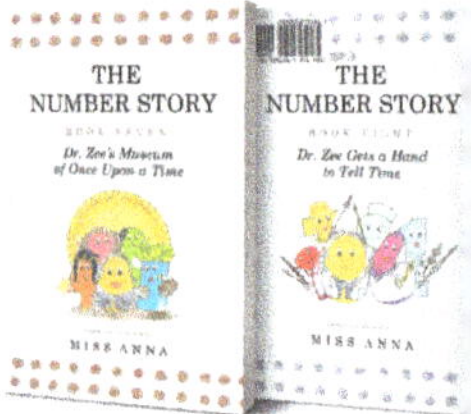

Number Story 1 & 2
isbn: 978-0-996216-48-7

Number Story 3 & 4
isbn: 978-1-945977-01-5

Number Story 5 & 6
isbn: 978-1-945977-06-0

Number Story 7 & 8
isbn: 978-1-949320-40-

For more Miss Anna books to love,
visit us at

www.missannabooks.com

Numbers are working hard all over the world!
Come Travel the World with Us!